OUTRAGEOUS L.A.

OUTRAGEOUS L.A.

■ **Photographs by Robert Landau**

▶ **Text by Robert Landau & John Pashdag**

● **Chronicle Books**
San Francisco

Book and cover design:
Thomas Ingalls & Associates
Designers: Gail Grant
and Thomas Ingalls
Typography: Design & Type

The Burning House photograph
on the cover appears through
the courtesy of Universal Studios
Tour® in Universal City,
California.

Eve Szurky tries on glasses at
L.A. Eyeworks

Metropolis on Santa Monica
Boulevard and company car

Printed in Japan.

Library of Congress Cataloging
in Publication Data

Landau, Robert.
  Outrageous L.A.

  1. Los Angeles (Calif.)—
Description—Views. 2. Los An-
geles (Calif.)—Popular culture—
Pictorial works. 3. California,
Southern—Description and
travel—Views. 4. California,
Southern—Popular culture—
Pictorial works. 5. Photography,
Artistic. I. Title. F869.L843L36
1984 306'.09794'94   84-5903
ISBN 0-87701-291-1

Chronicle Books
870 Market Street
San Francisco, CA 94102

Acknowledgments:

I would like to thank:

Victoria Westermark
James Phillippi
Edward Ruscha

for their invaluable contributions
to this book. I also want to thank
the following people for sharing
their thoughts of L.A. with me:

Jerry Dunphy
Robert Fitzpatrick
Barbara Goldstein
Robert Irwin
Eric Moss
Larry Niven
Henry Rogers

Contents

Preface

I was majoring in sociology in college when I discovered that photography was a very legitimate, valid way of studying people, of portraying people in culture. That aspect of photography is very much a part of my work. I want to say something about people and the way they live, even something about how buildings and cultural artifacts reflect the kind of values people have in this society.

Our culture here in Los Angeles, and to a great extent the whole country, is really based on popular notions. When you drive down the street, you don't see many monuments to great artists, or philosophers, or even religious figures. What you see is McDonald's golden arches, or Bob's Big Boy with a statue out front, or a giant chicken. Without passing moral judgment, what I'm saying is that these things honestly do represent our culture and our values.

I use a journalistic approach in that I don't preconceive what an image is going to be. I rarely decide in advance what, aside from a given area or event, I'm going to photograph. I try, rather, to keep an open mind, to respond to that which I actually find. I try, like a journalist, to look at something and convey a sense of the truth about it. I've also learned the value of being concise from journalism; by eliminating unnecessary information and reducing an image to its most essential elements, the communication is more precise.

I don't use any mechanical trickery. I don't manipulate the photographic process. I don't collage elements. I don't double expose. Everything is straight photography. There's a trend currently in photography that you have to manipulate a photograph to make it art—you have to paint on it, you have to change it, or you have to build something and photograph that. I use a simpler approach that relies on how you look at things, a very pure application of photography. To me, the real art of photography is that it can quite beautifully, eloquently and accurately capture and present a very refined image of visual information.

Of course, the notion that photographs don't lie is misleading. They tell a select truth. A photographer manipulates how his subject is perceived through various choices—what to show, how to present it, which moment in time to capture it, what to include or exclude in a frame. Without really manipulating the photographic process, the photographer still has a great deal of control over the final result.

I make a conscious interpretation in what I shoot only in the sense that I anticipate that something is going to happen and place myself in a position to catch it. There's a certain amount of luck involved, and some planning, but basically I rely upon my intuition. Later on, in the printing, I'll make a more conscious effort to select the images that really say what it is I want to say about the subject.

There are so many things competing for attention in the contemporary landscape—street signs, billboards, automobiles, people, various kinds of architecture—that there is a visual overload. People eventually learn to stop seeing, to block out a great deal of what's around them. What I'm trying to do as a photographer is to focus on certain everyday sights that most people might not see, and say, "Here, look—this is what it really looks like. I didn't invent this, I didn't paint it—this is a photograph of what exists. Examine this and see what it means, see what it says about L.A."

Having lived most of my life here in Los Angeles, looking at it, driving through it, pondering it and photographing it, I've reached only one solid conclusion about this city, and that is that it simply defies definition. L.A. is obvious and unpredictable, beautiful and ugly, a true 20th century city and no city at all.

I have no doubt that a thousand books could be written about Los Angeles, each describing or portraying one of a thousand different cities, and all of those cities could be L.A. Therefore, it would be ridiculous to suggest that this book, this group of photographs and statements in any way "defines" the L.A. experience. Rather, what it does is celebrate some of the possibilities available within the L.A. spectrum. I've tried to select elements of Los Angeles that reflect its diverse character and capture a sense of the spirit that makes it truly unique.

"*There is no* there *there*."
                    Gertrude Stein

There's No Place Like L.A.
by John Pashdag & Robert Landau

Miss Stein, of course, was referring to the Northern California city of Oakland, but her famous quote has been applied to the Southern California city of Los Angeles so often that we might as well claim it as our own and use it to define L.A. as well. And define L.A. it does: there is no *here* here. To try to pin down Los Angeles, to declare that is indelibly *this* or irrevocably *that,* is to risk being made a fool of by the very nature of Los Angeles, which is at once all-encompassing and ever changing, like a giant amoeba that constantly alters its structure, size and shape. One cannot pin down Los Angeles any more than one can put one's finger on an amoeba and hold it in place. Is Los Angeles Hollywood and the movies, or is it the beach? Is it a center for learning, a capital of world finance and trade, or a focal point for the chanting Krishna worshippers and other exotic religious sects? Is it Disneyland or is it downtown, the Wilshire business district or Knott's Berry Farm, Middle America or Chinatown, yin or yang, fair or foul, frick or frack?

The nearest thing to an answer, of course, would be all of the above, plus a lot more. The one identifying characteristic of L.A. is the impossibility of defining L.A. It's a crazy hodgepodge of culture made up of bits and pieces of everything from Old Spain to New Wave, so that even the most astute, most broad-minded sociologist must approach the place with the restricted acuity of one of the proverbial blind men facing the elephant for the first time. It's simply too big and too varied to take in at once.

That given, it's still possible to concede that certain parts of the Southern California elephant are more unusual and more interesting than the rest. From the annual Doo Dah Parade in Pasadena to Hollywood Boulevard on Halloween night, there are things that the Los Angeles area has that you just don't find anywhere else. Those are the things that make L.A. unique, and while concentrating on them

may not give any more comprehensive or authentic a view of the city than concentrating on other subjects would, such an approach does provide the most legitimate description of what L.A. is all about.

Take color, for example. Color, more than an embellishment, is an integral part of Los Angeles. Colors here aren't earthy, they're vibrant, alive, pulsating with the supercharged energy of light reflected off the most outrageous pigments on any artist's color chart. From purple storefronts to electric orange sunsets, colors in Los Angeles *demand* attention, crashing in past your iris, grabbing your retinal cells by the handful, and screaming, "Listen to me, Jack—I'm talking to *you!*" And listen you do; there's no way to even begin to describe L.A. without taking its colors into account. Both the natural and the artificial colors have something that would seem to many people unreal, but they *are* real; they're just brighter and more intense than colors anywhere else.

Consider, also, Los Angeles weather and other natural phenomena, including those which insurance companies irreverently refer to as "acts of God." Gorgeous blue skies and golden sunshine have become so traditional for New Year's Day in Southern California that each year, thousands of Rose Bowl and Rose Parade viewers in colder parts of the country turn off their sets and loudly announce, "Pack up the kids, Martha, we're moving to Californy." Then they get here and it rains for a month. Not just light drizzles, but torrents that make Somerset Maugham's descriptions of life in Malaya in the monsoon season seem like local news. To top it off, in the middle of one week-long rainstorm last winter, a number of communities in Southern California were shaken by small earthquakes, and a tornado tore the roof off the Los Angeles Convention Center, while another stranded hundreds of shirt-sleeved passengers for hours on the Skyride at Disneyland. Bob Dylan once wrote, "I'm used to four seasons,

California's got but one." Then he moved to Malibu, where mudslides, earth tremors and brush fires are a part of everyday life. He doesn't write like that anymore.

Just as singular as the L.A. weather is the response it gets from those who live here. The generally beautiful weather that Los Angeles enjoys most of the year certainly does create California girls with their tropical tans and golden hair, as well as their masculine counterparts. In the warm weather, people are a lot freer in what they can wear, simply because they don't have to wear as much, which in turn leads to more people taking better care of their bodies, because more of them are on display. The fact that you can go swimming in the ocean in December or play tennis outdoors nearly every day of the year adds immeasurably to the lifestyle here, while contributing at least a little bit to the sense of unreality that's permanently in the air; the absence of three or four months a year of continuously harsh winter weather creates a kind of endless summer, with its correlative feeling of being on vacation all the time.

When the natural disasters do strike—when the hills burn, the buildings topple, and the cliffs come tumbling down—there's a feeling that such events are a small price to pay in return for the rest of the year. The disasters take on a festival feeling, giving people something a little exotic, something unusual to talk about, a common bond. Even the people who live in the danger zones—the hills that seem always on fire, the beaches that erode away—take their precarious positions in stride and often with pride, laughing in the face of danger and misfortune, shrugging off the occasional loss (that's what insurance and government disaster aid are for, isn't it?) and—usually—rebuilding in exactly the same spot as before. The only lasting danger is that over the years, their friends might tire of hearing the same old story of how the catamaran came flying through the second-floor window, or how someone knew his house was in trouble when he saw his hot tub floating out to sea.

The sense of fantasy, or at least alternate reality, created by Angelenos' response to the weather pervades other aspects of Los Angeles as well. There are individuals who come here and create their own little fantasy worlds, like Walt Disney, or Grandma Prisbrey with her Bottle Village, or the doctor in Malibu who built his castle on top of a hill. If you look around L.A., it's hard to find any buildings or remnants from much before 1900. When you don't have much in the way of built-in heritage, as you do in an Eastern or European city where culture has been established for centuries, there's not so much to either build on or react against; you're on your own in terms of developing an identity or character. This lack of heritage gives Angelenos a strong sense of freedom, and that lack of restriction—combined with the fact that L.A.'s wide open spaces make it possible for you to be who you are without getting in your neighbor's way—allows people here to indulge their fantasies on a scale unparalleled anywhere else. You can walk down the street dressed like a turkey and people will barely turn their heads. The uninhibited use of imagination is expressed in every facet of life in Los Angeles: the way people dress, the way they paint their cars, build and decorate their homes, advertise their businesses, display their goods. Nowhere else on earth does the Id reign so supreme.

If the city's space and lack of roots are the spark and tinder that set off fantasies, the presence of the movie business and the Hollywood dream are the winds that fan the flames. In many people's minds, L.A. *is* Hollywood. There's a tremendous amount of romanticizing that goes on about movie stars and the possibility that you could give up your job in the Midwest and come out here and become famous, a tremendous feeling that anything is possible, both in the movies and in the place where the movies are made. Once you're out here, of course, it's a different story; becoming a superstar takes just a little less work than becoming president of General Motors and just a little less luck than being born Prince of Wales. Still, the fantasy persists, remaining as big a lure as the New Year's Day weather reports.

The whole notion, in a way, is misleading; Hollywood is really just one more part of Los Angeles, and if you go to the corner of Hollywood and Vine expecting to find glamour and magic, you're in for a rude surprise. Nonetheless, even in contemporary times there is a need for mythology, and Hollywood writes a great deal of it, creating heroes and influencing trends all over the world. Clark Gable appeared barechested in *It Happened One Night,* and millions of American men stopped wearing t-shirts; Brando appeared in his torn, dirty t-shirt in *A Streetcar Named Desire,* and the same millions put them back on. On a higher level, while there might be a child somewhere in the Western world who's unfamiliar with E.T., an older, equally cute, if more earthbound, character named Mickey Mouse is known by all. Hollywood creates far more than just shadows on a screen and pigments on a piece of celluloid film.

Nor is Hollywood the only part of Los Angeles that creates worldwide trends. Because L.A. is the home of so much mass media, the amount of media attention focused on the place is enormous, and things that get started here get picked up by the newspapers and television and go out across the country very quickly, whereas if something new happens in Pittsburgh, it takes a long time before you find out about it in L.A. A place like New York is like the Louvre in Paris—a testament to what was—but L.A. is the personification of Tom Wolfe's The Church of What's Happening Now. The latest heroes, the latest movie stars, the latest trend—disco roller skating, cold pasta salad, Valley Girls—it all starts here and spreads across the country with a speed that would do bubonic plague proud. It only has to be new and exciting and different. Life can be grey and dismal, the economy can be going to hell, and something like a new way of making ice cream cones comes along and provides a distraction—it's an amusement, and L.A. is very good at that. Whether Los Angeles is as superficial as it's often made out to be is something for history to decide, but history will remember that superficial or not, L.A. was nonetheless created for the most part by real people making real choices about how they wanted to live their real lives.

History will also remember that L.A. loved to laugh. There's a sense of humor here that comes in part, perhaps, from repressed reactions against the more outlandish expressions of personal fantasy and freedom one sees on the streets, but also in part from equally repressed feelings of admiration, of I-wish-I-could-get-away-with-that. The greatest part of it, though, comes not from deep-seated psychological feeling but from a conscious realization that it's just no *fun* to go around being gloomy all the time, that we're not here for very long and it's a beautiful day outside, so let's enjoy it to the fullest while we may. People here aren't afraid to make fun of or have fun with either themselves or their city, or to indulge their sense of humor in something as simple as painting your Volkswagen with zebra stripes, or something as complex as the Doo Dah Parade. One of the perennial favorites at the parade, which began as the Pasadena artists' community's reaction to the stuffiness of the Rose Parade, is the Marching Precision Brief Case Drill Team, made up of pinstripe-suited bankers from Pasadena itself, and one of the groups participating in the parade for the first time last year was the Newport Beach Dull Men's Club, a pride of middle-aged businessmen who marched in time to the muffled roar of their portable leaf blowers. Only in Los Angeles do you often get the feeling that you're living in a Joan Rivers monologue or a Monty Python movie; try to imagine the Doo Dah Parade, complete with bankers and Dull Men, taking place in Peoria, and you'll see what we mean.

Humor in L.A. can take the form of absurdist juxtapositions—bankers in the Doo Dah Parade, skiers at the beach—or, as a garish purple-flocked Christmas tree attests, it can just be downright intrinsically absurd. It can also take on a lighter, more whimsical quality, as in the L.A. Fine Arts Squad's mural of Venice Beach covered with snow. Much of Los Angeles art, in fact, deals in whimsy, whether it's Ed Ruscha's lithographs printed in gunpowder and tomato juice, or the murals along the flood control channel facing the Ventura Freeway, the only murals in any city designed especially to be seen at 55 miles an hour. It's not that L.A. artists aren't serious about their art; it's just that, like the rest of us who live here, they refuse to take *life* too seriously, that's all.

Los Angeles has been called many things by many people over the years, from a hundred suburbs in search of a city to the greatest city in the world, from lotusland to crackpotville to heaven on earth. While no one place—not even Los Angeles—can be all things to all people, Los Angeles comes close; with its size and diversity, it can offer anyone who takes the time to search through all its nooks and crannies nearly anything that person could possibly want. If there *is* anyplace like L.A., nobody's found it yet.

A Conversation with Edward Ruscha

Q. Why did you come to L.A. from Oklahoma?

A. The first thing I had to do was get out of Oklahoma. As much as I liked the place, there was no room for artists or inspiration whatsoever. This was 1956. I was attracted to going either east or west. At that time, and pretty much today, the East Coast was starched clothing and heating oil, while the West Coast was flexing biceps and health. This made the choice relatively easy. Didn't all Okies with mattresses on their cars go west, anyway? Beyond that, I seemed to be drawn by the most stereotyped concepts of Los Angeles, such as cars, suntans, palm trees, swimming pools, strips of celluloid with perforations; even the word "sunset" had glamour. West was hot. East was cold. This was new life. That was Europe. This city simply had a good story for itself, that's all.

Q. How does L.A. influence your work?

A. All my work gets affected by the things that attracted me to this town in the first place, together with the little twists in my character that motivate me. A heavenly mountaintop is not going to get the job done. This is it for me, at least for now.

Q. Is the "spirit" of the place still the wide open spaces—freedom kind of thing that brought you out here?

A. I think so. You can look at the sunset and see it here. There's something in the sunset. The East Coast has a sunset that is metallic—our sunset is more "glorious." Also, after I moved here, I found that L.A. tolerates any kind of behavior or life style, and that suited me fine.

Q. What about humor? Take the Fine Arts Squad mural of the Pacific Ocean at Blythe, after California's fallen into the ocean—do you think a piece of art like that, taking the greatest natural disaster that could befall the place and putting it up on the wall of a recording studio, could come out of New York?

A. I don't think so. I think that particular work is probably one of the best examples of art in the community—art being relative to the community. I know that painting and I've always liked it. It seems like there's a nail whose head has been hit, you know? Beyond that mural, I think that Chicano clothing and car styling are some of the most worthwhile contributions that L.A. has ever produced.

Q. Does L.A. appreciate and value its artists?

A. No, not particularly.

Q. What does L.A. value highly? What is held in high esteem here?

A. The freeways. Just so those cars keep moving. I'm a part of it almost every day. It's sort of like a rolling thunder parade, isn't it?

Q. How would you describe the L.A. environment? You can't really say it's beautiful.

A. Well, I think it is. It's not beautiful exactly on the surface; it's beautiful in a kind of folklore sense, and it's quaint in the sense that it has not been as hard-hit by bulldozers and blacktopping as other communities have.

Q. Do you like driving?

A. I don't dislike it. You can turn on the radio and the radio becomes the sound track for what you see out the window. And somehow I get more from doing this in Los Angeles than I do in another city.

Q. What about earthquakes? Do they frighten you?

A. No. Earthquakes, I think, are kind of gentle and friendly. I have not been wronged by an earthquake. I don't particularly *like* earthquakes—sure, there's a certain helplessness when they happen, but if I see this window rolling back and forth like this, there's nothing I can do except laugh.

Q. What makes L.A. unique?

A. It is the ultimate cardboard cutout town. It's full of illusions and it allows its people to indulge in all of these illusions. It's a siren calling me. I always have to come back to this city—I don't know what it is. There is plenty about this town that aggravates me, but I'm a victim of magnetic attraction.

Q. What about the cultural mix?

A. I think everybody is gradually mixing here. There doesn't seem to be rampant prejudice here, or a reluctance to get together, as far as cultures go. We all want to live in the center of the picture postcard. A hundred years from now there will be some gorgeous mono-ethnic race living here. It's probably as it should be.

Q. What do you do for recreation?

A. Drive and fish.

Q. Do you think painting will ever be an outdated medium?

A. I don't think so. It may not be the medium of the future, though. I think there might be some form in moviemaking that can actually begin to say more than what a painting can say. It certainly has potential. That's why I like movies so much, because I think they do have a certain power of expression that two-dimensional things can't have. Painting and movies both suffer from mediocrity, though, but one will never actually replace the other. Movies are the result of involved collaboration, while painting is completely free and singular.

Q. What does the term "pop culture" mean to you?

A. Does that come from "popular?" That probably means anything that's happening today.

Q. Does that give an ephemeral side to our culture?

A. Yes. It's sort of instant this and instant that. And nothing really stays around. So what's wrong with that?

Q. People tend to look at it and assume it's very superficial.

A. Superficiality can be profound and funny and worth living for. I mean, everything's ephemeral when you look at it in its proper focus. It just happens more quickly in L.A.

OUTRAGEOUS L.A.

Once upon a time in the '50s, details like these Necco-wafer circles were considered "moderne"; now they're considered camp.

The patriotic arches of Pioneer Chicken. With few statues in Los Angeles, the local pigeons make do with plastic pop monuments instead.

▶ The Great Western building at
the intersection of Wilshire and
La Cienega boulevards doesn't
seem to know that International
Style buildings are supposed to
be rectangular, not oval in shape.

With dozens of neighborhood centers scattered around L.A.'s 450-plus square miles, most Angelenos go downtown as seldom as possible, which means they miss seeing such gems of architecture as the Eastern Columbia Building, a magnificent art deco skyscraper on South Broadway. Built to house the headquarters of a furniture and clothing store in 1929, the building serves today as the home of the Los Angeles Conservancy, a society dedicated to the preservation of local landmarks.

■ These archways could be part of
a temple, but they're really part
of a temple of science—the
Griffith Observatory. If they look
familiar, it's probably because
they formed part of the backdrop
for the knife fight between James
Dean and Corey Allen in *Rebel
Without a Cause.*

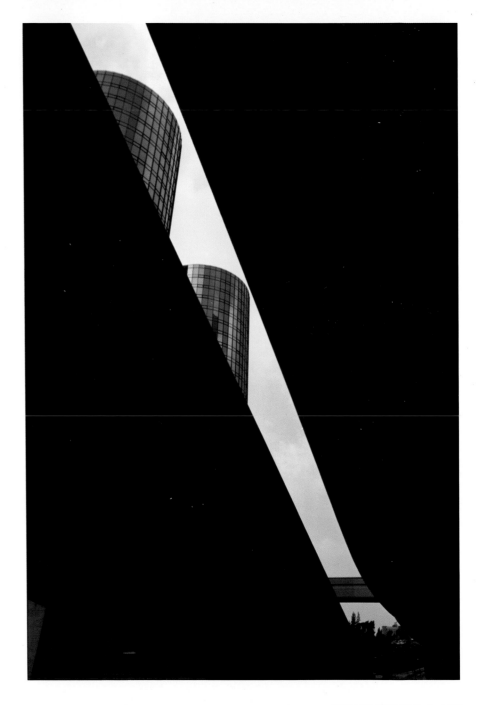

The Bonaventure Hotel, designed by John Portman of Hyatt Hotel fame, opened for business in 1976. Seen here from beneath a freeway overpass, it lends a futuristic touch to the changing downtown skyline.

■ The brilliantly art deco Pan Pacific Auditorium, a true Los Angeles landmark, sits in disrepair amidst a newly landscaped park. Current plans call for the auditorium's facade to be preserved and restored, as part of a new, multimillion-dollar hotel and recreation complex.

▶ The exterior of a Mexican bar near Alvarado Street hints at the gaiety inside.

A coffee shop near the airport reaches for the sky with a late '50s version of space age architecture.

● The idea that L.A. has something for eveyone has no clearer expression than in a row of street-corner news-boxes. If you can't find a newspaper to your liking in this town, you're just not trying. The ones here, on a street in Hollywood, offer everything from swingers' guides to religious literature to the *Los Angeles Times*.

■ Weathering from the desert sun has made these beams at a Palm Springs motel seem less cheery than they must have been when they were newly painted.

● There's no getting away from cacti in Southern California, even at the beach. These brightly painted metal saguaros are part of a children's playground in Venice.

■ Painting buildings pink isn't just an L.A. phenomenon; the original color scheme of the Parthenon in Athens was equally gaudy. The Athenians, though, would never think of painting the Parthenon that way today, while here in Los Angeles, someone would slap a coat of paint on it in a second.

▶ The swimming pool, like the palm tree, has moved into the realm of L.A. iconography.

Many small apartment houses tend to look alike, except in L.A., where all it takes to bestow individuality is a bucket of paint—or, better yet, two or three.

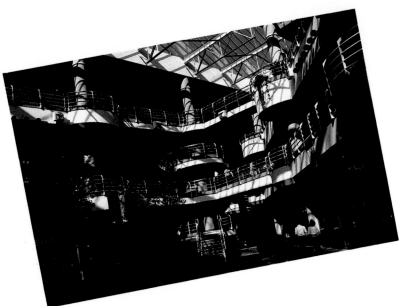

Immortalized for better or verse by Moon Unit Zappa, the Sherman Oaks Galleria was indeed the birthplace of the Valley Girl.

When an Easterner thinks of trees, he thinks of maples, oaks, and elms; when an Angeleno thinks of trees, he thinks of palm trees. These geometrically spaced specimens in the courtyard of the Wells Fargo Bank building downtown present a more formal picture than most, as palm trees in nature don't often engage in close-order drill.

Has the saying "a man's home is his castle" ever been more appropriate? This one was built by a local general practitioner in 1975 in the hills above Malibu, and has been advertised for sale for the paltry sum of $5 million.

▶ The Villa dei Papiri was buried by the eruption of Vesuvius in 79 A.D. Some 1,900 years later, J. Paul Getty supervised by phone from England the construction of this replica of the first-century Roman country house. He never did visit the villa, but you can, on his foundation's Malibu ranch.

■ The Brand Library, tucked away in a typical residential neighborhood of Glendale, is one of the Southland's best kept secrets. The Brand family left it to the city of Glendale as a library, and it offers a highly specialized collection of art- and music-related books and an art gallery.

▶ A gnarled old palm tree in Beverly Hills takes a different approach to the more traditional vertical stance. Trees like this one are often homes to Beverly Hills' two most common wild animals, Mexican parrots and German roof rats.

Long before New Wave fashion came into vogue, Los Angeles had a thing for pink. This salmon wall and fuchsia flowers are in the staid Wilshire district, where numerous insurance companies, banks, and other conservative firms make their homes.

The majestic-looking date palms in Indio and other desert communities are the only Southland palms that bear edible fruit, an attribute celebrated annually at the Indio Date Festival and camel races.

■ The interplay of local architecture and nature creates a typical Los Angeles composition.

A lathed roof lends this cactus display a zebra-striped shading. As might be expected, the Southland offers several fine cactus gardens, including ones at UCLA, Beverly Hills, and the Huntington Gardens in San Marino.

► The real palms' shadows weren't enough for the designer who painted this stylized image on the wall of the Santa Monica Place shopping center, thus illustrating a common trait among Angelenos: the inability to leave nature's designs alone.

Bending nature to man's will
sometimes takes a formal
direction.

With its tall palm trees, cool swimming pools, and patios Palm Springs is the stereotypical image of L.A., accentuated. The dry climate and hot desert sun make the springs a year-round playground for local hedonists and, on spring and Labor Day holidays, the mecca of school-age good-timers.

▶ In a Hollywood movie theater lobby, promoters of a new film attempt to get publicity by going after the world's record for hot tub stuffing. About 50 volunteers made it into this one, which didn't help the film any; more people would rather sit in a hot tub than watch someone else do it.

No, not outer space messages. At this Psychic Fair booth for past-life meditation, the distances perceived are of an entirely different kind.

In L.A., the star mentality pervades even physical exercise. Here Jane Fonda leads an exercise class at her Workout in Beverly Hills, where the status-conscious can have their backs as well as their egos rubbed.

● Knott's Berry Farm really did start out in 1934 as a homey roadside berry stand, but if you want to bring in the tourists today, you need something a little zoomier. Montezooma's Revenge, which goes from 0 to 55 miles an hour in five seconds before turning you and your stomach upside down, will suffice.

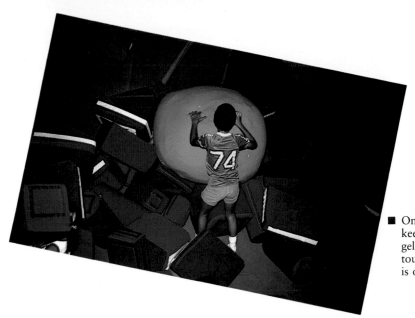

■ One of the major concerns at most museums is how to keep kids from touching everything; at the Los Angeles Children's Museum, the task is to *get* the kids to touch everything, a job at which the Sticky City room is obviously successful.

Water slides, bumper boats, go-carts, miniature golf courses, video game arcades—leisure time in L.A. takes on a thousand meanings. Never have so many spent so much in pursuit of so little.

The annual Pioneer Pass Golf Tournament attracts an odd blend of sportsmen/masochists who come to play it where it lays—in this rugged terrain, through cactus and over rock.

Forget Wrigley Field and Connie Mack Stadium; baseball's *fun*, fellas, and who can have fun in a ballpark that looks like a factory? Paint it pink.

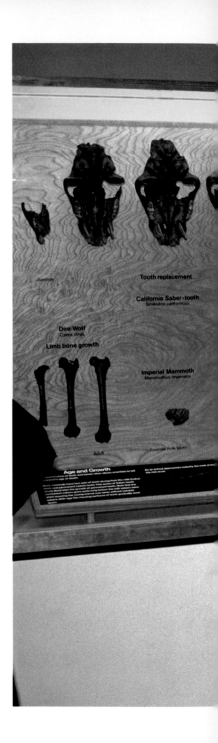

■ The La Brea Tar Pits have yielded the bones of thousands of Ice Age animals, like this reconstructed mammoth, that fell into the sticky pits, sank, and were preserved for thousands of years. Often, found next to the bones of a mammoth or prehistoric deer or ground sloth are the bones of a saber-toothed tiger or other predator that was trying to snare the tar-imprisoned animal when it too slipped and fell in. The Page Museum, behind the tar pits, exhibits many finds. Animals still get stuck and sink into the tar; what will our descendants thousands of years from now make of the remains of the cement mammoth, do you suppose?

▶ The Greeks had mythological figures, who were immortalized in bronze. In Los Angeles, we take Nancy Sinatra and make a figure of her in wax. It's very fleeting, this fame thing. If you were Zeus, you were a god year in and year out. If you are Nancy Sinatra, you had your turn and now it's somebody else's.

● In the tradition of such stars as Lassie, Mr. Ed, and Flipper, these performers at Hanna-Barbera's Marineland rarely miss their cue and usually make a big splash with visitors to the seaside aquarium on the Palos Verdes Peninsula.

In Los Angeles, betting on what's real and what isn't is a sucker bet. These are real actors who are pretending to be ordinary people trying to be actors.

■ The Grand Canal in Venice is a vestige of the Italianate dream of Abbot Kinney, who in 1900 dredged sixteen miles of canals along the stretch of coast he named Venice, and even imported gondolas and gondoliers. By the '70s, the city wanted to fill in the canals, but new residents kept them safe for ducks.

It's always hard to tell what's real and what isn't in Los Angeles, but the problem is compounded at places like Knott's Berry Farm. Here a shooting gallery nestles up against the side of a plaster mountain.

L.A. is somewhat short on monuments; we don't have parks filled with pigeon-dropping-covered statues of Civil War generals. We do, however, have the High Desert Christ Monument, erected single-handedly by Antone Martin, a retired pattern maker, in Palm Desert, east of Los Angeles on the road to Palm Springs. A little farther along the same road is Southern California's only life-size dinosaur, benignly standing watch over the patrons of the Wheel Inn Truck Stop. It took Claude Bell eleven years and $225,000 to build the complex here, his lifelong dream.

Even in Los Angeles with its "anything goes" architecture, some houses stand out more than others. The Beverly Hills Witch House was built as the office for the Irvin Willat Motion Picture Studio; it's easy to guess what sort of pictures Willat made. Then in the '20s Willat married and lived in the structure. In the '60s the house appeared in movies once more, as John Gielgud's house in *The Loved One*. Since then it's had a sedate life as just another almost-ordinary Beverly Hills residence— although it's still a favorite with local youngsters on Halloween.

People often think of Disneyland as a garden of innocence, forgetting that Walt Disney knew how to scare the bejeezus out of small children with characters like the evil queen in *Snow White* and film sequences like *Fantasia's* "Night on Bald Mountain." Come upon suddenly, this skull is guaranteed to give any preschooler a very un-Mickey-Mouse-like thrill. Al Stoval designed this garden of hippos, a few of the more than 800 botanically sculpted trees that surround his Inn of Tomorrow motel, across the street from Disneyland.

Even if you can't make it to the Rose Parade (and with New Year's Eve the night before, who can?), you can still see the floats in a nearby park the next day.

■ With all the fishing piers and barges along the South-land coast, fresh fish is available for the taking for anyone who's willing to make the trek to the beach. At a small marketplace near the Newport Beach Pier, a fisherman prepares his catch.

Murals cover dozens of walls in Los Angeles, but few relate to the buildings whose walls they cover as directly as this one on the side of a pet shop in the Crenshaw district.

The Doo Dah Parade is quintessential Los Angeles. What began as a light-hearted response to the pompous Tournament of Roses Parade has turned into an event of increasing notoriety with no official rules—other than no damn roses. Here anyone can be a star, including the normally crusty, the generically crustaceous, and the somewhat less classifiable.

● This shop's window display unintentionally reflects a cliché about inhabitants of the West Coast: great bodies, no minds.

Just as Europeans might feel weighted down by Europe's rich culture and long for something fresh and new, people here long for a rich and established heritage. Creating our own culture is what the display of Michaelangelo's *David*, an instant artifact that sticks out like a sore thumb, is all about.

Masks are very big in Los Angeles. People in L.A. quickly and eagerly respond to any opportunity to dress up or act out. Here a Hollywood magic shop window offers a sinister selection of alter egos for Halloween; at other times of the year, the masks are less obvious.

This could be an average night on Hollywood Boulevard, but it happens to be Halloween—open season for those who like to become or survey the unusual. Even the younger participants, like this young fan of the rock group Kiss, attract stares. Some of the boulevard regulars who don't wear masks are just as scary.

From the days of Aimee Semple MacPherson, Los Angeles has been the country's major center for religious cults. The Hare Krishnas (officially known as IS-KCON, the International Society for Krishna Consciousness) are among the most successful, with temples and schools where children as young as four or five shave their heads, wear saffron robes, and learn to chant the names of the Hindu lords. This older believer wears a topknot, so that Krishna can yank him into heaven when his time comes.

■ One way to keep from feeling lost in a place as big and as shapeless as L.A. is to pay closer attention to your roots. For the Hispanic community, that often means going back beyond the Spanish-Mexican settlement of El Pueblo de la Reina de Los Angeles to the great Aztec Indian culture of Aztlan. By telling the world who her ancestors were, this girl, performing at the annual Street Scene festival in downtown Los Angeles, is telling herself something about who she is.

At the annual Festival of the Chariots at Venice Beach, robed Krishna devotees pull elaborately decorated two-story chariots along Ocean Front Walk in a smaller version of an annual festival held in Benares, India.

Olvera Street is the oldest street in town, a remnant of the pueblo founded in 1781. After 150 years as a dirty, run-down alley, in 1930 it was restored. Now it's crammed with taco stands and vendors selling cactus candy and South of the Border souvenirs—some classy, most tacky. Events here range from the annual Blessing of the Animals to Mexican folk dancing.

● Evoking tribal celebration, Los Angeles's Gay Pride Parade fills the streets with revelers and observers.

▶ An English landscape architect designed Echo Park in 1899, modeling it after a garden in Derbyshire that was trimmed with a lotus pond. Now L.A.'s large Asian community holds the Lotus Festival and Dragon Boat Races here each spring; the rest of the year, it's a Latino gang hangout. The melting pot bubbles over.

At events in the Southland it is often the spectators who bring color and focus to the goings on. At the Asian community's Lotus Blossom Festival, a woman shields herself from the sun with a bright parasol, and a little girl gets a lift to see over the crowd. The fashionable canine, clearly prepared for shaded viewing, seems to need a lift, too.

On Rodeo Drive in Beverly Hills, where every other car is a Mercedes or a Rolls, and every language but English seems to be spoken, the already frenzied shopping scene reaches a feverish pitch just before Christmas.

The San Diego Freeway from Sunset Boulevard, at sunset.

● Sunsets like this are thankfully rare, even in Los Angeles; the colors are intensified by the presence of ash in the atmosphere from a brush fire in the Santa Monica Mountains.

There's no mistaking the direction this sign on a Sunset Strip liquor store wants you to go.

There's not much neon in L.A.—it's more of an Eastern item—but what's there is as colorful as the rest of the city. This motel is in Anaheim near Disneyland, which probably explains why the neon Musketeer appears to be some sort of buck-toothed rodent.

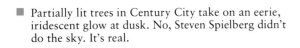 Partially lit trees in Century City take on an eerie, iridescent glow at dusk. No, Steven Spielberg didn't do the sky. It's real.

The fairytale image is in Los Angeles, in Chinatown, a fact that would be more readily discernible if nearly all of the lanterns that once covered the bare light bulbs weren't missing. If the Chinese restaurant were elsewhere, its owners likely would not have thought of trimming the pagoda in neon. Somehow, in L.A., it's more honest this way.

When the Beverly Hills Electric Fountain at the intersection of Wilshire and Santa Monica boulevards was first turned on in 1931, the dancing waters and the constantly changing array of colors caused traffic jams of gawking motorists. The city considered dimming the lights for safety's sake, but fortunately the motorists became used to it. A kneeling figure praying for rain tops the fountain.

● "Welcome to L.A." A plane approaches Los Angeles International Airport amidst the splendor of a Technicolor sunset.

▶ PAINT ... your car. This sign is its own best advertisement.

■ Ordinarily, the ant on the wall might be truckin' *toward* McDonald's golden arches, but he's just spent all his money on clothes at Ants n' Pants next door.

When a local radio station designed this billboard, it's unlikely they planned on the palm tree hairdo. Nature strikes back in mysterious ways.

■ At the busy shopping intersection of Fairfax Avenue and Wilshire Boulevard, a model on a Calvin Klein billboard hungrily eyes a Johnie's Fat Boy burger.

▶ One pop icon eyes another from his Hollywood bus stop bench. If Clark Gable's smiling, it's probably because he knows that more people know who he is than the fellow on the right.

■ Whoever painted the exterior of
this club near downtown obviously didn't know that pool
halls are supposed to be dim, col-
orless places. In the companion
photo, the sign states only what is
obvious about Los Angeles's
character. The vivid natural environment existed first, but those
who settled here expounded on
its colorful theme, and now
whether the people or their constructed surroundings are the
greatest source of vibrant hue is
moot.

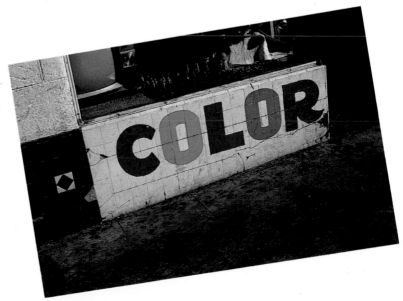

● Spotted along Los Angeles's streets and highways are Paul Bunyan-sized figures hawking everything from tires and mufflers and donuts and burgers to a car lot, stadium parking, and a veterinarian's services. The paint peels from icons once famous in Saturday morning cartoons, but others fare better. The structure that is a bar on Alvarado Street is a now rare example of "programatic" architecture—that of buildings shaped like objects or animals—and is valued by aficionados as a gem of its genre.

You don't necessarily have to be a millionaire to create a dream house. An eighty-year-old woman known affectionately as Grandma Prisbrey, seen outside hers, has been building this monument to individual expression from discarded materials since 1955. Called "Bottle Village," this series of structures north of Los Angeles houses her collection of found objects, which includes hundreds of pencils and dolls along with thousands of unusual bottles from all over the world. Prisbrey constructed the buildings out of cement, bottles, a few old car headlights, and anything else she could get her hands on. Her unique juxtaposition of diverse elements creates an unforgettable and sometimes surrealistic folk art experience.

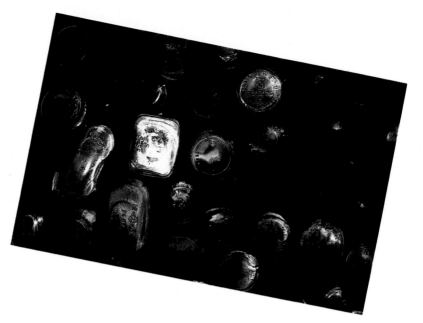

● From within, the walls at Grandma Prisbrey's Bottle
Village are reminiscent of stained glass windows in old
churches. The path outside, leading through the village, is a crazy quilt mosaic of tiles and found objects.

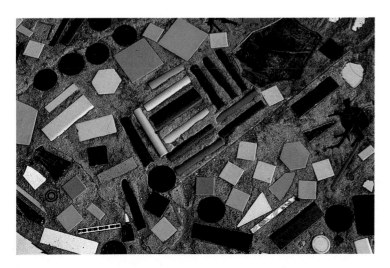

The Virgin of Guadalupe, patron of Mexico, stands out in this basketful of miracles in a souvenir shop on Olvera Street.

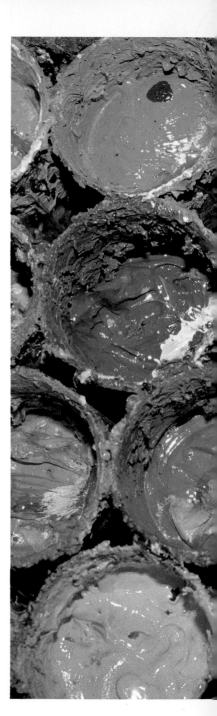

Farmer's Market began in the Depression as a handful of independent farm stands; today it's a tourist trap with dozens of stands and shops selling everything from donuts to salt water taffy to souvenir leather billfolds.

This palette of exuberant Los Angeles color will end up on Foster and Kleiser's billboards around the city.